Table of Contents

Welcome to the Program

It took me over 15 yrs to develop what is now "The Transformation Method". It all started with me adopting a Wild Horse and learning how to communicate and train this wild animal. Through the years of constant improvement from coaching and valued mentors I started to develop a Scientific Method to release the fear and insecurities of these wild horses.

This Scientific Method created a question, "If this type of transformation is possible in a Wild Horse to go from a completely fear based from an instinctive reaction to finding absolute calmness in an entirely different reality, how can I do this myself? How can I make a transformational experience for me?" That one question took me four years to find the answer. You are about to experience that answer, The Transformation Method is designed by Mother Nature and hidden within the Wild Horses, based on Scientific principles specifically for YOU! What will the Mustang teach you about you?

Sincerely,

West Taylor

Wild West Mustang Ranch
Science Based Horsemanship

1

Meet West & Kami

West and Kami have been together for over 35 years, they have 4 children and 9 grandchildren!! You will often hear them say that they are on their fourth marriage and have never been divorced. They have both experienced massive life-growth opportunities, including West's own near-death 2 different times, leaving Kami to adjust and make her own life transformations. This power couple truly discovered "*The Transformation Method*" together and have implemented it directly into all growth areas of their life including the release of 25 year old traumas together.

From West

West Taylor, once a businessman and IT communications contractor was forced to let go of all the worldly identity of who he was, his business, his vehicles, his toys, his house, his standing in the community, all to search out a new way to live, a way to seek peace, joy and connection in his life. Some say he is a horse whisperer... he will say he chooses to listen to the horse by building a relationship based on safety with the horses. West has had two major near deathexperiences that shifted who he is and how he chooses to live his life.He spent 15 years drowning his life in alcohol when a grizzly bear intent on killing him in the backcountry of Alaska changed him forever. Some say your life flashes before your eyes right before the end. West said all he could think of was his family and how out of alignment his relationships were and all of the things he had not yet experienced in his life. After this life awakening moment West took five years off to spend every moment with two wild mustangs he adopted from the Bureau of Land Management.

West identified with something in these once wild and free horses that were now in pens in captivity.They appeared to be in the same mental state as he was. Removed from everything that was once safe, not sure of his future and scared.

West now lives on his family ranch in Fremont Utah where he and his wife Miss Kami of 35+ years hold retreats and workshops where West and Kami teach this Transformation Method. Together they share their life experiences through their passion and purpose to heal the relationships of humans and horses through life coaching sessions in partnership with the once Wild Horse and the healing power of the drum, meditation and sound healing.

West says a horse can not lie... all they know is truth, living in the now... moment to moment and if you're open to listen... the horse has a message for you. What will the horse teach you about you?

From Kami

West and I started this Transformation Method based on West's life lessons with horse training. I have watched him work with horses for many many hours and it has taught me a lot about me and how I was showing up for myself and also in my relationships with others, with money, with my body and so much more. I have learned to change my old stories and it has changed me and my life in all areas. I have lived much of my life based on old beliefs and stories I was told and now I am choosing to create the life "I" want to live by pre telling my story. I love and believe in this work and want everyone to be able to love the life they live.

Creation of The West Taylor Method

It took me over 15 yrs to develop what is now "*The Transformation Method*". It all started with me adopting a Wild Horse and learning how to communicate and train this wild animal. Through the years of constant improvement from coaching and valued mentors I started to develop a Scientific Method to release the fear and natural insecurities of these wild horses. This Scientific Method created a question, "*If this type of transformation is possible in a Wild Horse to go from a completely fear based instinctive place to finding absolute calmness in an entirely different reality, how can I do this myself? How can I make a transformational experience for me?*" That one question took me four years to find the answer. You are about to experience that answer, The Transformation Method is designed and proven by Mother Nature and the Wild Horses, based on Scientific principles specifically for YOU!

It all started with what felt like the worst experience of my life! The repo man had taken everything of value, we had sold everything else, we were vacated from our family home. My worst nightmare was REAL and happening right now. This was September 2008. My once thriving IT communications business was crumbling and falling apart with the devastating housing market crash. I lost it all, my business, my house, my money, my lifestyle and most of all I lost my identity to myself!

I moved my family from the once thriving community of St. George Utah into my recently deceased grandfather's ranch house in a very small rural ranching community in Fremont Utah. I felt alone, I felt defeated, I felt I had no direction, no purpose. I had just lost everything I thought I was, and now I stand here at the rundown family ranch with my wife of 25 years starting our life completely over at the age of 40.

All I wanted in my life was a feeling of safety, a feeling of peace. How, where do I find this?

I attended a Wild Horse adoption event, there I found the Mustang, seemingly alone just like I was. Without much thought I adopted my first Wild Horse, brought this 3 year old mare back to the ranch, somehow I thought that this horse would fix my life, would make me whole again. Little did I know that this mustang would completely redefine me as a man.

I had purpose, I had a horse to figure out how to train. I was going to ride this horse one day! I had a dream! This was the beginning of many many struggles as I had zero experience in training horses.

Somehow my intuition guided me along, introducing me to two of my life changing mentors, Janiece Wilson and Dr. Stephen Peters. Janiece taught me the expert ways of handling horses, how to ride, how to be balanced, and how to really work with the horse. Dr. Stephen Peters a NeuroScientist taught me all about the neurochemicals and the autonomic system of fight flight, the sympathetic nervous system and rest, relax, the parasympathetic nervous system and how these neuro chemicals can increase our ability to learn and how they can inhibit your ability to learn. Then he shared the biggest gold nugget of my horse training career, these same neuro chemicals and autonomic systems exist within the horse. Figure out how to manage the horse's autonomic system and you will forever change how you work with horses and people.

Janiece Wilson

5

Dr. Stephen Peters

Drum Ceremonies

West and I live in Southeastern Utah on a wild mustang ranch. We are advocates for the wild horses in America and adopt and train them, this is West's passion and purpose. I call him my mustang man!

West and I attended our first drum circle together in 2011 at a retreat and that is when we fell in love with the heartbeat of the drum. It was a really cool experience being a giver and a receiver at the same time while drumming that evening. I heard the voice of the drum and felt the power of healing through sound, vibration and frequency. We purchased 2 drums and as an artist I went straight home to put artwork on them. This has become "*MY passion and purpose!*" Through lots of trial and error I came to know that I was to be a drum maker. I often questioned who would buy a drum from a blue eyed blonde haired white girl. This was a story I quickly let go of as people were excited to have a drum made by me and to have me paint custom artwork for them. My ancestors led me to the ways I was to go about teaching and making drums for the people of this generation. We hold drum ceremonies at our Ranch and have seen many miracles come from these experiences. I also make many drums and paint custom artwork on them and teach the ancient art of drum making. One of my favorite things about drumming is that it's an active meditation! Drumming creates a community and brings others together for healing.

There are many things that happen to bring us out of alignment every day. The good news is drumming and sound healing brings our bodies back into balance.
The benefits of sound therapy include Physical vibration can relax tight muscles. Drumming resets your nervous system and can literally bring the autonomic nervous system from fight/flight in the sympathetic to rest, relax and restore in the parasympathetic almost immediately. Science has also proven that daily drumming can boost the immune system and create an overall sense of happiness and wellbeing. Many of the guests that come to the ranch say how great they slept after we drummed them around the campfire before bed. This has become part of our daily life and for us a way of being.

Kami Sue Taylor
White Feather
Wild West Mustang Ranch

1 Stories

Humans are the only species on the planet that define their safety based on stories. Stories from our past, stories from our ancestors and even stories that simply are not true.

2 Experiences

Our experiences are the opportunity to create change, to create a new belief, to create transformation. Our experiences are our struggles, it's not supposed to be easy!

West Taylor
TRANSFORMATION METHOD

Self

This is who we are, or who we think we are. Our view of self is a combination of our stories and our experiences. We see ourselves based on the stories we tell and the experiences of our life.

3

Relationships

Our relationships with money, people, sex, success, exercise, nutrition, and nature are all related to how we perceive ourselves. Changing our stories will transform our lives!

4

What is the Transformation Method?

The Transformation Method is a very simple yet complex process, it's easy to do and it's even easier not to do! Us humans create our neurochemical reactions and responses based on our stories from past experiences and past stories about past experiences. This all happens most generally at a subconscious state, meaning we are not purposely telling ourselves these stories; they just happen at a level below our awareness.

These stories create our neurochemical responses, otherwise known as our feelings. We then take these feelings from our past experiences and start to create the same experience, it feels the same as last time, because we are allowing our old stories to dictate our feelings about something that hasn't even happened yet.
This is part of being human, it's just how we are wired. The good news is we can change this wiring, we can reprogram our stories to create new different experiences, different feelings about the experiences we are having and the experiences we are going to have in the future.

This rewiring all starts with becoming aware that we are living our life based on stories from our past. With awareness we can begin to change our stories, we can tell a new story about an old experience and this will begin the process of creating a new story to create new experiences. Us humans define ourselves based on our past stories and experiences, we call this our personality, we often even believe that we are just born this way and we cannot change our wiring. This simply is not true. We have the capacity to recreate ourselves, to rewire our personality into a completely different person. As we begin this process of redefining who we are we begin to create a new reality, a new version of ourselves living in a newly created reality. This is where we begin to create our new relationships with ourselves, with our loved ones, our friends and the reality that we live in.
Change your story and you can change your life.

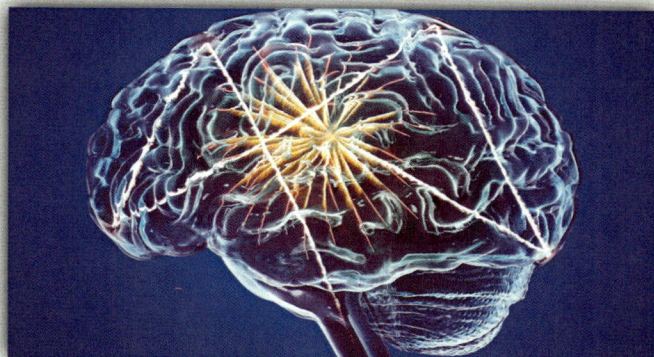

We Are Our Stories

Humans are the only species on the planet that use storytelling to create our reality. All other species live much more simply in the NOW moment. Everything that you are thinking about right now comes from a form of a story, maybe one that was told to you by your parents, perhaps a story that you told yourself at a very young age. Our culture is filled with stories. All of our holidays are celebrated from stories. Our history is a written story of the past, much of our own personal family history is handed down from one generation to another. Have you heard the story about mom's secret recipe for cooking a ham? The secret to the recipe is that you cut off each end of the ham before cooking. Then you rub the seasoning onto each end of the ham, then place it in the pan for cooking. This secret family recipe was handed down from one generation to another. Then one day the great grand daughter asked her great grandmother how she came to discover this secret to cooking the perfect ham. The great grandmother replied to her great granddaughter with laughter, oh my dear, there is no secret to cutting off the ends of the ham, that is the only way I could get the ham to fit into the pan!

Each time we tell a story, or allow a story to subconsciously be told to ourselves our body creates a neurochemical release, we feel these neurochemical releases as our feelings. When we hear a story or tell a story about love we feel the story in our body through the neurochemicals that the story creates. If we hear a scary story our body creates the neurochemical feelings of fear. This is all very normal autonomic behavior, where we allow ourselves to upregulate and create stress in our system. By believing that all these stories are true, or allowing these neurochemicals to dictate our behavior without any pause or slow down to fact check, to see what is really happening. To the body this upregulation can feel like the "*thing*" is happening, when in reality nothing is happening.

The horse is a great example of how fast this upregulation can happen. Wild horses have a very high "*self preservation*". To a wild horse EVERYTHING is a threat until proven otherwise. Its kind of like there is an internal story telling the horse that everything is unsafe until proven otherwise and should be cautious of everything at all times!

Finding Awareness

Our everyday language, the words that we think and speak are our stories. Each thought and each word spoken creates a neurochemical response in our body. Think about having a conversation with a friend, maybe you told your friend "oh I could never do that!" or "I am terrible at learning new things" each of these statements creates a neurochemical response, a feeling of truth inside of ourselves. Our autonomic system of fight flight and rest relax are influenced by the thoughts and words we speak.

Science has proven that we have up to 80,000 thoughts per day. Science has also proven that generally we go throughout our day 80-95% in an unconscious behavior. How many times have you driven to work or the grocery store and have been completely unaware of how you got there? You were on autopilot while driving to your routine destination. We go through our daily lives in this same unconscious behavior. This unconscious behavior is where our stories run at full speed without any conscious input from ourselves, we simply allow the same story to run automatically, the traffic is bad, the stop lights are too long, the road rage is getting worse, these are all stories that run automatically in the background of our consciousness. We allow these stories to be true simply by not being conscious of them. Same as the horse, everything is a threat until proven otherwise, everything becomes stressful in our lives until we become aware of our stories.

Once you find awareness of the stories you are telling...

How quickly can you hit the pause button?

The Pause comes right after you become aware.

A great way to slow down and be present is by using breath work. Box breathing is a simple technique we use when we become aware that our autonomic nervous system becomes up regulated *(stressed, anxious, cautious, concerned)* this could look like fear, anger, confusion.

What is box breathing?
Box breathing is a powerful but simple relaxation technique that aims to return breathing to its normal rhythm after a stressful experience. It may help clear the mind, relax the body, and improve focus. Box breathing, also known as the Navy Seal Breathing or four-square breathing, it is resetting the breath and is easy to do, quick to learn, and can be highly effective in stressful situations.

It involves these four simple steps, each lasting 4 seconds:

~breathing in for 4

~holding the breath for 4

~breathing out for 4

~holding the breath for 4

HOLD - 4 sec.
EXHALE - 4 sec.
BOX BREATHING
INHALE - 4 sec.
HOLD - 4 sec.

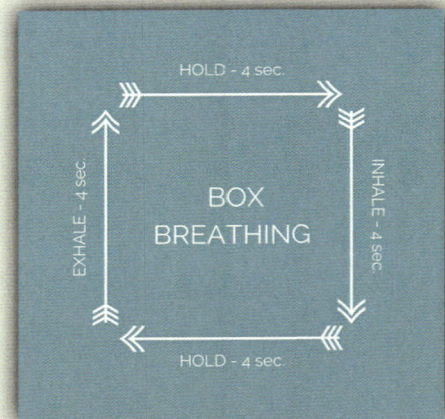

People with high stress jobs, such as soldiers and police officers, often use box breathing when their bodies are in fight-or-flight mode. This technique is also relevant for anyone interested in re-centering themselves or improving their concentration. This breathing technique can take your autonomic nervous system from the sympathetic *(fight, flight, freeze or fawn)* to the parasympathetic *(rest relax restore)* in a matter of minutes.

Are you aware when you are holding your breath?
How about when your breathing becomes elevated or shallow? Did you know that we automatically breathe in different ways when we are under stress, some people get really stressed at the doctor or dentist, when they are sad, when they cry, when we rest, when we meditate, when we sleep, even when we are having sex.

Notes

Finding the Pause

Finding the pause button of our autonomic system is critical to our mental and spiritual safety.

The PAUSE is simple to do and also so simple not to do.

Pausing to ask ourselves "*Is this a story?*" simply slow down and really allow yourself to be with the story, meaning to be engaged with the story rather than let it flow through your subconscious as an unchecked truth. Many of our stories are just words, phrases put together by our friends and family, our co-workers. My wife recently went to Costco for groceries. She mentioned this to our daughter who had just returned home from her trip to costco. My daughter stated, "*they were all out of milk and eggs!*" both items were on my wifes list of things to get, she went anyway. My wife called me later and told me the story of our daughter complaining that costco was completely out of milk and eggs, like it was the first step to the end of the world, costco was out of milk and eggs! My daughter was absolutely concerned about her family's food supply! Her mind definitely was telling her a scary story about food for her family!

By the time my wife got there she said that the Costco guy was placing several pallets of milk and the eggs had also been restocked, saving our human existence. How many times do we allow a story to affect our emotions? Our feelings? Our plans? When we slow down and hear the information being told as a "*story*" that may or may not actually be true we can take back the control of our autonomic system response of flight/flight. We can balance ourselves, this is called Self Regulation.

By pausing, by slowing down the story you can take a real look at this information. Perhaps some of it is true, perhaps none of it is true. When we slow down our autonomic response we are taking back control, we are taking back the influence of our neurochemical response system. This Is how we manage ourselves, this is how we Self Regulate while under pressure. Pausing and slowing down is how we stay safe! A great way to slow down and be present is by using breath work. Box breathing is a simple technique we can use when we become aware that our autonomic nervous system becomes up regulated (*stressed, anxious, cautious, concerned*) this could look like fear, anger, confusion.

Fact Checking

Fact checking is a simple and effective way to check out some of the autonomic stories that run wildly through our subconscious and conscious state of mind. It really only takes but a few questions to "*get some clarity*" on a story. Take for example, my daughter was shopping at Costco and Costco was all out of milk and eggs and my daughter was relaying this story to my wife and how concerned she was that COSTCO was running out of food! Simply slow down this story, let's take a look at it. Lets ask a few simple questions to ourselves about this story. Did my daughter ask any Costco employees if they would be restocking milk and eggs? Nope, she just made her own observation, and then her autonomic system kicked into fear mode and started telling her a story about not having food.

She then retold this story to how many people? At Least one, my wife who now has a story in her mind that Costco is out of milk and eggs, maybe she cancels her trip to Costco, maybe she gets a bit concerned herself and starts to worry about not getting her supply of milk and eggs. This one simple "*untrue*" story caused the release of stress hormones for sure in my daughter. Cortisol and adrenaline are now influencing her mood, her feelings, her emotions, she is now more stressed than when she went to the store. All this stress builds up over time, and somewhere someday it's going to come out. The healthier way to release stress is to minimize the amount that gets into our system. Fact checking our stories is a super antidote for stress relief! Don't allow it in to begin with.

Breaking down the story by asking a few simple questions.

Is it possible that this story is not even true?
Yes, nobody asked the grocery store about the inventory of milk and eggs.

Am I going to change my plans based on a story that is possibly not true?
Simply asking this question presents the reality that the story could not be true, so making a conscious decision to continue with my plans is lowering my stress response and internal stress levels.

How important is it to me to verify this story right now?
By simply slowing down it is pretty easy to create a "*plan B*". If the grocery store is actually out of milk and eggs I can choose to stop at a different store or simply go without at this time. A conscious decision will keep my stress system more balanced.

Remember, humans tell stories, it's just how we operate, chances are whatever you are hearing is likely not true at all, or at least has some major untruths woven inside the story.

Fact Checking

Pick a simple story from your life within the past few days. What did somebody tell you? What story did you allow to automatically make itself true inside of you?

Write your story below

_____
_____
_____

Lets ask a few questions about this story.

Is it possible that this story is not even true? *(Write out some possibilities that this story is not true)*

_____
_____
_____
_____

Am I going to change my thoughts and feelings based on a story that is possibly not true?

_____
_____
_____
_____

How important is it to me to verify this story right now? Is it easier to assume that the story is not true and continue with my plans?

_____
_____
_____
_____
_____

Remember, humans tell stories, it's just how we operate, chances are whatever you are hearing is likely not true at all, or at least has some major untruths woven inside the story.

15

Transformation Starts in Our Experiences

Our experiences equals action. When we put our new story under pressure we do this in our experiences. If we allow our same old story to play out the same way it always has in our experiences we are rewarding our old story which actually makes it even stronger. We can use this same practice to create and tell a new story. By putting our new story under pressure in our experiences and holding to the new story even when it's uncomfortable through the experience, this is how we make change in our lives, change in our beliefs about ourselves.

Each thought that we have in our mind, our neurochemical system will create a feeling that is associated with our thoughts. This process is how our autonomic system creates safety for us. It takes work, it takes struggle to make a change in your autonomic system. By crafting, by writing, by telling ourselves a NEW story we will begin to create a new neurochemistry of belief, a new neurochemistry of ourselves. Taking this new story into our experiences is how we rewire our autonomic system. We must put the new story under pressure, to hold strong to the new belief we are creating. This all happens during the struggle,this happens in the same place that your old story would talk you out of doing this hard thing. You literally have to break apart the old wiring, the old programming and rewire yourself to this new story, this new belief. Neurons that fire together wire together in your experiences.

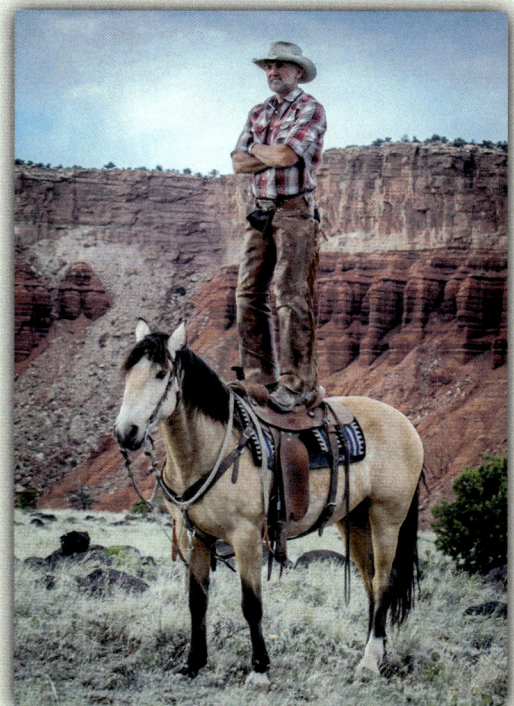

16

Notes

Pre-Tell Your Story

Pre tell your story before your experience. This is like ordering your food at a restaurant. You tell your waitress what dish you would like, you describe how you would like it cooked, you describe the side dishes you would like, you place your drink order to have your most favorite beverage. You are pre telling what food you want at that moment. You don't sit down and simply tell the server to bring you anything from the kitchen. You consciously slow your mind down and read over the available options and make your selection.

You can do the same thing with your life! Pre tell yourself what it is you want out of each experience you have. Here is another example, this one is personal to me, this actually is a real life story about me.

Typically my wife does all of our grocery shopping, it's something she likes to do, she enjoys the variety and creation of dishes she can make for our meals. I on the other hand don't really enjoy walking around the grocery store looking at all the options and seeing what type of a meal I could create, it's just too much for me mentally. If our meals were left for me to decide we would have pre made meals with very few choices. So Kami does all the shopping and she always invites me along with her, sometimes I go and most times I don't.

This is the old story I told myself about shopping, It's not really my thing, I don't like driving through the parking lot looking for a parking spot, it causes me stress, I really don't like walking around the store, food is just not interesting to me, I don't care what is "*on sale*", or "*in season*" food and shopping are simply not an enjoyable experience for me.

However I do love spending time with my wife so when I do go to the store with her I put on my best face and endure through the experience. I find myself scrolling through social media to distract myself from the stress and anxiety of all the options and all the people. This also causes me to be very distracted from having a pleasant conversation with my wife while we shop.

Here is my new story I tell myself each time Kami asks if I want to go shopping with her. Yes, I would love to drive you to the grocery store. During the drive I tell myself to notice how beautiful the sky is, how puffy the clouds are, and how pleasant it is to spend some quiet time with my wife in the car. When we get to the parking lot I am excited to find a parking spot, I tell myself it's OK to park in the very back of the parking lot, this eliminates the stress of finding a parking spot.

As soon as we are out of the car I grab my wife's hand and make a conscious effort to lightly caress her hand as we walk from the back of the parking lot to the front doors, I thank her for inviting me to spend this time with her. As soon as we get inside the store I go immediately to the candy bar aisle to get my most favorite candy bar from when I was a kid. My grandma Jenny would always buy me a Snickers candy bar when I would go to the store with her. After I have my favorite candy bar I head over to get my favorite drink, which currently is a green tea.

Kami has already got her cart and I meet her near the produce section to begin shopping. I snack on my favorite candy bar and enjoy my favorite drink while I follow her around the store pleasantly discussing the topics of our life. Yes I eat my snacks while we are still in the store. It always brings a smile to the cashiers face when I hand her my empty Snickers wrapper and a half empty can of Ice Tea to scan.

I pre-tell this story each time Kami asks me to go shopping with her. I have done this so many times now that when she asks I automatically say yes as I feel very relaxed and even a bit excited to have my favorite treats while I enjoy her company shopping.

Pre-Tell a New Story

The Experience

In order to change your STORY about an experience you need to imagine what that new story could look like, pre tell a *"new story"* here & practice saying and doing this story the NEW way during the experience.

_____
_____
_____
_____

Ex·pe·ri·ence:
   NOUN: Practical contact with and observation of facts or events.
                    "she had already learned her lesson by painful experience"
Similar: involvement in, participation in, contact with, acquaintance with, exposure to, observation of, awareness of, familiarity with, conversance with, understanding of, impression of, insight into.
   VERB: Encounter or undergo (*an event or occurrence*).
                    "She is experiencing difficulties"

Dis·trac·tion:
   NOUN: A thing that prevents someone from giving full attention to something else.
Similar: Diversion, Interruption, disturbance, Intrusion, Interference, Obstruction, hindrance extreme agitation of the mind or emotions.

The Distraction

Distractions keep us from feeling the pain or discomfort of our experience

Make a list of your distractions. *(Remember in my previous story, I would use my phone and social media to distract myslef from being present. Some others examples might include eating, stress cleaning, shopping, binging on Netflix, etc.)*

_____
_____
_____
_____
_____
_____
_____

Old Stories to New Experiences

When we allow our old stories from the past to dictate the neurochemistry of a new experience that has not happened yet, we become victims of ourselves, victims of our old stories. This process can go on FOREVER!

If we want to make changes in our beliefs, if we want to transform our lives to a new belief we must change our stories before the new experience. This will begin the process of changing our neurochemistry away from the stress and untruths of the old story and start to create new neurochemistry BEFORE the new experience. You may even want to rehearse the new story several times, telling yourself what the new experience will be like in the future. Allow yourself to feel the new neurochemistry BEFORE you even have the experience. This will begin the process of rewiring your autonomic response system to the new story.

Take a few minutes to write out an old story you would like to change.

Start with the Old Story.

_____
_____
_____
_____

Take some time to creatively tell a new version of your old story. Be creative, add some FUN concepts to your story, like eating your favorite candy bar :)

New Story.

_____
_____
_____
_____
_____

Now all you have to do is put this new story under pressure, create an experience for you to take your new story into your reality. Hold strong to your new story all the way through your new experience. This is how we make changes to our autonomic stories. This is how we change our reality.

Notes

Self Regulation

Self Regulation is the super power to strive for! Self Regulation is what happens when we are able to monitor, to be aware of our autonomic system and the current stress level we are under. This awareness of our bodies neurochemical "*feelings*" is how we can begin to use this super power of Self Regulation. When we feel ourselves ramping up, becoming anxious and stressed we can bring ourselves back down to a reasonable and engaging state of mind or state of the body.

Self Regulation comes from within, it is inside of us. WIthout Self Regulation we blame the exterior world and the exterior events, the exterior people and circumstances in our lives for all the stress and anxiety we have. When we are stressed our autonomic system prepares us for fight flight, our heart rate increases, our respiratory system kicks in for a race with short shallow breaths, our hearing becomes dampened, our eye sight becomes very narrow and focused, our motor system is engaged and on high alert for action, our cognitive abilities, our good decision making capacity is diminished by ⅓. Our entire autonomic system is triggered and prepared for FIGHT FLIGHT, all because we were not able to consciously take over control from the inside. We allowed our stories, our exterior events and circumstances to take over. This is all great and needed if we are really being chased by a predator. All this happened because somebody cut you off in traffic, or somebody said something to you, or you saw somebody from your past!

One of my favorite tools for Self Regulation is breath work. Becoming aware of my breathing. As soon as I notice my system starting to elevate I focus my attention on breathing. Box breathing is a very widely used tool by many people who are in high

stress environments, from military special forces to martial arts and people in everyday life at the grocery store. It's a simple and very effective tool to reverse all the high stress responses of our autonomic system. Breath in for four counts, hold for four counts, breath out for four counts, hold for four counts, repeat.

INHALE 4 SECONDS

HOLD 4 SECONDS

Box Breathing

HOLD 4 SECONDS

EXHALE 4 SECONDS

This breathing sequence resets the autonomic system out of flight fight, you are taking back control of your breathing. Your autonomic system will reset because you obviously are not being chased by a predator if you are breathing with this much purpose and focus. You heart rate will return to normal, your eyesight will return to a wider perspective, your hearing will become more aware and softer, your voice will lower in tone and intensity, your cognitive ability to make good decisions will be restored, all of this will change your autonomic neurochemistry out of stress hormones of cortisol and adrenaline to the relaxing hormones of dopamine and serotonin.

NeuroChemical Rewards

When we allow our old story to create our neurochemistry we are actually creating a reward network that will create a stronger story of negativity. Each time the old story is allowed to run its course, to talk you out of doing the thing you are actually receiving a dopamine reward for NOT doing the thing. Each time this opportunity comes up and the old story talks you out of doing the thing you are creating a reward network of *"not doing the thing"*.

By telling the new story first, then following through with the new experience you are moving the reward from *"not doing"* into the energy of actually *"doing"*.
It will take some practice, some repetition to get this reward moved away from the old story and *"not doing"* over to the new story and the new experience. It feels hard and confusing at first. Over time and a few new stories and new experiences this new neuro network of *"doing"* will become the default neuro network replacing the old *"don't do it"* network.

An example of how we reward ourselves by *"not doing the hard thing"* would be similar to saying, *"I am going for a walk around the neighborhood today"*. As we all know, life tends to get in the way of doing these new hard things. We allow ourselves to be distracted by our day to to day chores and tasks. Like doing the dishes or doing laundry. Our internal story may say something like, *"you don't have time to go for the walk around the neighborhood today, you have to do the dishes and clean the kitchen, plus you have several loads of laundry that is not going to do itself!"* So you fall back into your old way of being, you do the dishes, you clean the kitchen and you even get the laundry done. All of this creates a reward system because you feel good that you did the things, the dishes, the cleaning ect...so you are in essence rewarding yourself for *"not doing the hard thing"*. So here is one way we can move the neurochemical rewards around. Tell yourself you will do the dishes and clean the kitchen and you will even do the laundry....AFTER you take time for you to do the hard thing, to go for a walk around the neighborhood FIRST. This will create the behavior reward of dopamine for walking around the neighborhood, so that the next time you tell yourself you're going to walk around the neighborhood you will have a pre built reward waiting for you which will make it easier to do the hard thing as you have now been rewarded for doing the hard thing. Repeat this process over and over until it is so easy to go for a walk around the neighborhood BEFORE you get busy and distracted with all the other daily tasks!

Awareness of You

Let's take an honest accountable look at ourselves. Who we are today is a reflection of our past stories and past experiences all stacked up on top of each other. Nothing "*wrong*" with who you are today, it's just a fact, you are a stack of stories and experiences period! No shame, no guilt, no should have done things differently! You are exactly where you are supposed to be right NOW!

Embrace your past stories and experiences, they have kept you safe from so many things that you didn't know you could handle. Now that you are becoming much more aware of who you are and what you can create yourself to be today, you may want to change a few things as you go forward into the rest of your life.

You are going to move forward in your life either way. From this "*now*" moment you can go back and retell some of your old stories from your past, you can create a new neurochemical "feeling" of that old story. That old story has served you well up to this point in your life, embrace it, thank it, love it and release it with your new story as you begin to create your new experiences.

You are who you are today based on the stories and experiences that have created your beliefs you hold to be true today. Change your stories and you will change your life, you can literally change your reality!

A new beginning.........

7 Elements of Self

As you study Health and wellness in any genre you will find a common theme, that common theme is BALANCE! This is also very true in horsemanship. When working with horses I have to constantly be checking for balance, too much in any one area leads to the horse being out of balance, not physically out of balance, I mean emotionally balanced. The horse must be balanced so it can handle pressure, stuff in life, stuff in its environment. I make a very clear protocol to do everything on both sides of the horse, it's pretty standard in the horse industry that riders always mount and dismount from the horse's left side. This is not due to the horse's preference, rather it comes from most humans being right handed and right side dominant. If the horse is only handled from its left side then the horse will naturally be more fearful and reactive of things on its right side, simply due to the "*out of balance*" due to how the horse was handled. We humans are a lot the same way. If we are not clearly working in several areas of our lives to create this balance we can become very unbalanced, very unstable. Anyone who has taken on any type of sport or major physical workout routine knows that nutrition is key to your physical success, without proper nutrition you cannot perform physically. Same holds true in the other areas of our lives. If we are not working to balance ourselves emotionally then we may also suffer in our spiritual growth. If we are not balancing ourselves financially, being accountable to our income, and being aware of our financial picture we may suffer mentally by creating so much worry and stress in other areas of our lives because we are not clear on our finances. The more balanced we are in these seven areas of our lives the more balanced our neurochemistry will be for life!

Take a few minutes to answer the below Seven Elements of Self quiz.

Are you aware of yourself? Your self talk? (*is it negative or positive?*) Have you ever been aware of how you speak to yourself in the mirror? Write out some of the "*self talk*" that you hear when looking in the mirror.

_____
_____
_____
_____
_____
_____
_____
_____
_____
_____

How are you balancing these 7 areas of your life daily?
Rate 1-10 (1 being poor and 10 excellent)
*possible ways to work on self in these areas

1- Emotional: _____
*read several pages of personal growth listen to self help podcasts

2- Physical: _____
*go for a walk, 45 min exercise daily, join a gym or take a fitness class, yoga, stretching or moving your body, aware of your body and is it in any pain?

3- Spiritual: _____
*be quiet with self a few minutes each day, nature, drum self or meditate, believability in a new modality or energy

4- Relational: _____
*say hello to a stranger or smile at someone, reach out to someone on your mind, compliment your partner, positive self talk

5- Financial: _____
*do 1 thing every day to prioritize spending or saving, check on your bank account, research ways to invest, give or donate, life insurance, buy somebody else's drink

6- Mental: _____
*make a checklist, be aware of self talk, create art or journal your day,

7- Nutritional: _____
*drink ½ your body weight in water daily, only consume unrefined sugar, limit alcohol intake to 1-2 days a week or focus on creating healthier eating habits

Total: _____   (possible being 70)

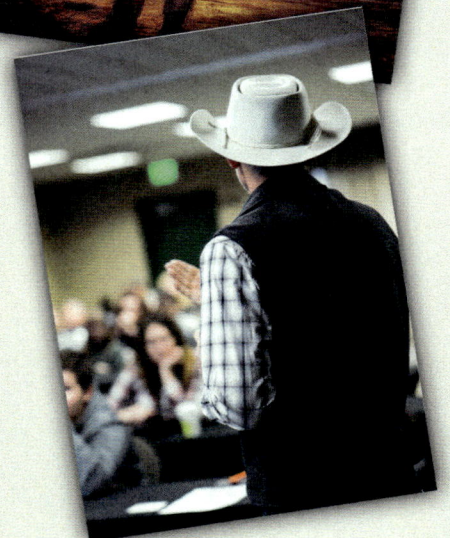

Are you taking care of you in all areas of your life?
If not, why? What story is holding you back?

_____
_____
_____
_____
_____
_____
_____

What areas could you improve on?

_____
_____
_____
_____
_____
_____

Write down a few ways you neglect yourself.
*Procrastinating fitness, ignoring promptings, avoiding out of fear, etc

_____
_____
_____
_____
_____
_____

I neglect myself by...

_____
_____
_____
_____
_____
_____

How does this make me feel?

_____
_____
_____
_____
_____
_____
_____

Whats 1 limiting belief or story you tell yourself?
(Example could be... eating healthy is too expensive or I don't have time to exercise.)

_____
_____
_____
_____
_____
_____
_____
_____

What would you like to change this story to?
(No matter the cost, I am worthy of eating healthy! My physical health is worth whatever time it takes! I can prioritize my time!)

_____
_____
_____
_____
_____
_____
_____

Remember to create a **NEW** experience to go with the new story!

Letting Go of the External

In my work with wild horses it took me several years to really figure out why the horses would be so jumpy, so sketchy so flighty in an environment that they had been in many times. This was early on in my learning and working with horses. Example, we had a mustang mare named June at the ranch. I was her first and only trainer, she was very wild and skittish when she got to the ranch. I put her in the pasture with some other mustangs and gave her several weeks to adjust to the new herd and living space. There is a beautiful little stream of water that runs through the west side of the pasture. The horses love to play in the water, jump across from bank to bank. I watched June as she engaged with all these playful activities, I watched her one day pawing and splashing in the water, simply enjoying her time.

A few weeks later and I had her where I could lead her on a halter and lead line, so I took her for a walk out in the pasture, down to the small stream to the exact spot I had just a few weeks ago observed her pawing and playing in the water. I thought how great this was going to be, she would easily walk right through the water I thought. Well I got within about 5 feet of the water and she stopped, not another step! I coached her, I tried different angles, I tried pulling her, I tried pushing her, I tried all the tricks I had at that time, nothing worked. I could not get her to enter the water at all. I was so perplexed, I didn't understand why she could so easily play in the water just a few days before when she was out with the other horses and today she would not even get close to it.

What I know now is that she didn't feel safe on the inside when she was with me, I had not built that internal sense of safety while she was in relationship with me. It had nothing to do with the water and had everything to do with her level of safety on the inside.

Ask yourself what environments or which people do you feel the most uncomfortable in?

_____
_____
_____

Now that you have identified where and with whom you feel the most uncomfortable, you have also identified the areas of your life where you do not carry a sense of safety internally within yourself. As you build your internal sense of safety the above environments and people will have less and less effect on your sense of safety.

Safety is Internal

When we don't feel safe on the inside it doesn't matter what environment we are in or who we are with, if the answer to the question "*AM I Safe?*" is not answered on the inside we will struggle to control everything on the outside to try to create our safety, the trouble is, there is simply just too much on the outside that we will never be able to control thus leaving our question of safety unanswered, which is an answer of "*No, you are not safe*".

Safety is an internal perspective, when we believe we are mentally safe on the inside our external environment will become so much less stressed as we are not seeking to control everybody and every outcome, we can simply observe from an internal sense of safety and let life take its course. When you are feeling the most stressed and anxious, STOP, take just a moment or two and ask yourself, "*What am I trying to control?*" Is it something that is external? Most likely it is! Your safety and calmness are on the inside not the outside. This is a great time for some breath work. Take back control of your internal autonomic system. Box breathing is a great and very underrated tool. Breathe in for 4 counts, HOLD for 4 counts, exhale for 4 counts, HOLD for 4 counts......repeat until you are feeling more relaxed. This simple process will reset your autonomic system to a sense of safety.

It was several years and many horses later that I took this concept full circle. I had recently started another mustang, who had not had any training or handling prior to coming to the ranch. I had learned a lot over the last several years about down regulation, about creating safety as an internal concept to the horse. I had only spent a few hours with this new mustang, a few hours of relaxing and lowering the horse's autonomic system to a place of calmness and safety. Things were progressing along so nicely.

I took this mustang for a walk to the same spot that a few years earlier I had taken June to. We walked calmly together to the water crossing, without any hesitation I just stepped across the water and held the thought in my mind (*and we had done the work*) "*we are safe*" and I stepped across the water and didn't look back, this mustang easily stepped right into the water and even wanted to paw and play a bit while we were there! I have repeated similar processes like this with many horses all with the same outcome, if the answer to the question "*Am I Safe?*" is answered in the autonomic system on the inside anything is possible!

Story Cards

We will be making a version of Melody Ross truth cards. Kami and I are certified through Melody's course and have found so much healing for "*self*" in making art. Let us introduce you to the value and experience of "*Art Therapy*". You are going to be creating your own story card. A story card is a simple cut and paste style of journaling. The idea is simple, you cut out a few images from old magazines or from images you have printed from the internet. The first set of images you are going to collect are images from a negative or old story that you want to "*re-tell*".

   1. So first decide which story from your past that you want to work with.
   2. Select a few images that help to represent that old story.
   3. Cut out some words to help you to "*tell*" that old story from magazines or the examples we included.
   4. Paste your images and the words onto the story page to represent your old story.

By taking the time to really put some images and words to your old story you may find it difficult to see this story out in front of you on paper. This story has lived inside of you based on fear for perhaps decades. This is OK, just be with it, just feel what it feels like to see this old story reduced down to a few images and a few words. This story has been larger than life for many years, this may be the first time you have actually put it into some perspective. This Is OK.

I should have started this when I was younger.

I am too old to learn new things!

I won't be good at it.

It will be embarrassing!!

Horses hurt people! I am afraid of getting hurt or bucked off

AGAIN

I AM sad when I choose not to ride!

Now turn your story card over to the new story. How could you tell this new story in an accountable and positive way (*see included story card example*).

As you seek out the new images for your story take your time, your brain is working to create new neuro networks to support your new story, don't rush this! Keep looking for just the right images. As you are creating the words for your new story, slow down, there is no rush. Give your brain and neurochemistry time to adjust as you are recreating how you are going to feel about this story. The time and effort it takes to find the images, to glue them to the page, to seek out the words to put on your new story card is how your brain and autonomic system are going to rewire you to your new story, your new experience. It's OK if this process takes you a few different settings to get it completed. It's OK to go slow and really sink into this process.

1. Create the new version of this old story, in your mind or write it out if needed.

2. Find and cut out some images of your new story

3. Find and cut out some words to tell your new story

4. Paste your new images and new story words onto your story page.

Hang this story card in your living space where you will see it everyday, Mine is on my bathroom mirror for me to see each time I brush my teeth. Each day you can rehearse, re-tell this new story to yourself. Each time creating a new neuro network, creating new neurochemistry which creates new feelings and emotions about your new story.

Have Fun!!

Notes

♥ What is a Truth Card™?

Truth cards are little cards that you can make for yourself as reminders of what is true about you and your soul, the things that can never be taken from you, because sometimes it is really hard to remember. Truth Cards are made by cutting and pasting words and images to a piece of rigid paper or cardstock, or an old playing card, or a rectangle cut out of a cereal box. They can be made out of just about anything. You can add other things like paper and fabric if you want to. The most important part of a truth card is the words, though.

When I created Truth Cards, I realized how important it was that they begin by addressing who you are. Because I don't know your name yet, friend, I have included a page of salutations to your soul to use on your Truth Cards. You are welcome to type out a sheet of paper with your own name on it to use, and I hope you do!

Here are some samples of what Truth Cards look like:

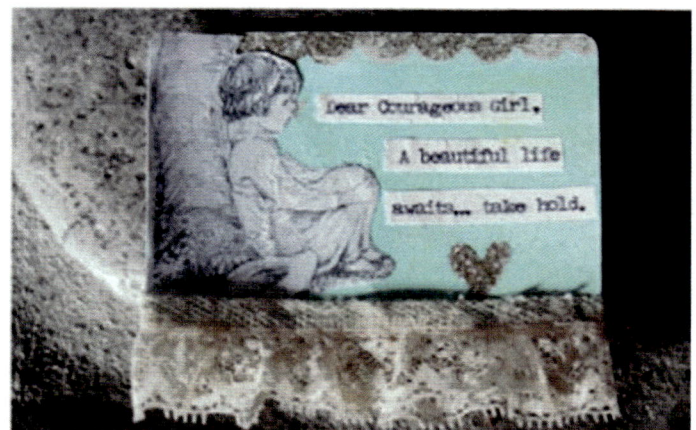

Why Truth Cards?

I created Truth Cards many years ago as a beautiful tool for my own soul work, to combat the lies we are fed every day about what is most important, who we are, who we can become, what we can accomplish, our value, our potential, our worth, what makes our lives meaningful, how & where we can find true happiness and how we can see ourselves and others.

Truth Cards came into being when I was going through a time of severe brokenness, confusion and loss of self. I needed to know the truth about myself and went on a very long quest to find it. One this soul search, I learned not only what was and is true about me, but what is true about all of us. As I was searching for what is true, I was inspired by my Truthteller (see The Red Carpet Rules to learn what Truthteller means) to write pages and pages of truths that were spoken to my heart. I started making Truth Cards as a way to remind myself of these truths.

Truth Cards have been so transformative in my own journey that I have shared them with others in just about all of my courses. Truth Cards have now been a catalyst of healing and change in countless lives and hearts all over the world.

♥ How to Make a Truth Card

1. Find a card or cut a card-sized piece of cardstock weight paper to work with. You can use playing cards, flashcards, even old gift cards!

2. If you want to, decorate or cover the background of the card with pretty paper, fabric, paint, wallpaper or anything lovely you can think of!

3. Read through the pages of truths provided in this kit. As you look through them, imagine they are coming from someone who knows all of you – your strengths, your weakness, your intentions, your secrets, your hurts, your struggles, your mistakes, your dreams, your victories. Imagine this person loves you no matter what and sees the very best of who you are and knows your potential.

4. As you are reading through the truths, cut out the ones that really speak to you. Sometimes they speak to you because they are the exact messages that you need to hear and sometimes they are messages that you wish you could believe about yourself. Whatever speaks to you, cut it out and set it aside.

6. When you are done cutting out the truths, you can assemble them into groups and even put some of the truths together into one message.

7. Once you have decided on the messages you want to use to make your Truth Cards, look through the salutation sheets starting with "Dear _____" and find the salutation that you would like to go with each message. You could also type out salutations with your own name and use those.

8. Look through the collage sheets to see if there is any art you would like to add to your Truth Card. You could also use photocopies of pictures of yourself and others, magazine clippings or any images that mean something to you. Cut out what you would like to use and place it with the cut-out truths that you would like to put with it.

9. Use a glue stick or some kind of paper collage medium, like Mod Podge and adhere your salutation, your truth message and artwork to the card.

10. You are done! Be sure to use these Truth Cards as a tool to speak to the deepest parts of yourself when you are feeling doubts or just needing a boost. And keep making them! You can never have too many Truth Cards!

PERFECTLY IMPERFECT

Age Gracefully

worth it

SHARE

BE A PIONEER

READY FOR THIS

love deeper

whole

ease

STAY STEADY

HEALED UP

START A REVOLUTION

focus

dream it

HOME IS BEST

together

good things are going to happen

listen

ask for it

no more excuses

MAKE TIME FOR IT

expect miracles

Let it go, let it come back... differently.
— Orly Avineri

see with new eyes

begin again

GIVE BACK

be an expert

LEARN IT WELL

a beautiful life

HAPPY

back to the basics

BE TRUE TO YOU

SHE IS GUTSY

MAKE A DIFFERENCE

SUPERSONIC

IT WILL HAPPEN

BE A MARVEL

it is time

LIVE LIFE

SHOW UP

just be

take care of yourself

time to flourish

reconnect

be gutsy

use your intuition

more fun please

wake up

Your life is meant to be something
more beautiful than you could dream.

You are brave enough.

You are strong enough.

Healing is worth the work it takes.

Keep going - no matter what.

Let pure love in - all the way in.

It is okay to cry if you need to cry.

Every experience has made you into
the phenomenal human being that
you are today.

It is okay to be afraid...
just do no let it paralyze you.

You are doing a great job -
keep it up.

You do not need to put so much
pressure on yourself.

Sometimes the healing seems to go
backward in the middle of going
forward - be patient with yourself.

You do not need to punish yourself-
please stop punishing yourself.

Everything will be good again-
it really will

You will laugh again.
It is good to laugh.
You will be whole again
It is good to be whole.
You will be happy again.
It is good to be happy.

You are so good inside

Let your best be good enough
because it is absolutely enough.

It is important to surround yourself
with souls who love you
and believe in you.

Let the healing happen.

Be willing to stop and rest.

You will get through this.

Look for the miracles-
they are everywhere.

So many people love you.

Let yourself have hope.

You are so much braver
than you think you are.

You are not alone on this journey.

You will heal-
you are healing right now.

Everything is going
to work out for your good.

it's okay to slow down and rest
you need to recharge your batteries.

Everyone has life seasons
there are good times and hard times -
there are confusing times - nothing
stays the same - be patient and try
to learn as much as you can from
each one - the seasons will change
again as soon as it is time.

It is never too late -
there is time for you
to be happy and whole.

* YES! YOU CAN CUT THESE OUT :)

Engaging With Your Reality

As we all go about our daily lives, working, socializing, recreating and relaxing we are seeing and experiencing our day to day reality based on the neurochemicals of our internal autonomic system. The safer we feel on the inside the safer we will experience our reality and thus the opposite is equally as true, the more stressed we are on the inside the more we will experience stress and anxiety in our day to day reality. The horses have proven this true to me beyond any doubt. The calmer their autonomic system is the calmer they see the environment and their reality.

The more annoying and stressful we find our reality to be the more we need to look internal for relief. Ask yourself, what am I thinking about? What am I telling myself right now? Remember our stories create our neurochemicals, when we feel the stress and anxiety that is our first clue to slow down, to take a look at the stories we are allowing to influence our autonomic system. Slow down and take some time to tell a new story, to relax and seek safety on the inside. Breath work is a critical tool to lower our autonomic system. As we regain control over our autonomic system we will start to see our reality in the same lens of calmness.

42

Investing in Relationships

Now that we have learned all about our stories, our experiences and ourselves, lets take some time to look at our relationships. This is not meant to be our relationships with our spouse or our significant persons. This is a look at how and where we INVEST in our relationships.

We invest in our relationships by the amount of time and attention we give to them. There are many areas of life that we humans have relationships with, here are a few.

- Love Relationships-spouse, partner, children, siblings, friends, lovers, ect..
- Food Relationships-fast food, healthy food, when we eat, what we eat, ect..
- Career Relationships-work hours, stress from work, bringing work home, ect..
- Finances Relationship-Time spent worrying about money, buying things, not buying things because you don't have the money, future retirement, savings, vacations, ect...
- Exercise Relationships-Time and attention to creating a stronger healthier body, being outdoors, having a weekly program, ect..
- Body Relationship-Awareness of your body, creating it to be what you want, proper nutrition, spiritual messages from your body, stretching and flexibility, ect..
- Sex Realtionships-Beliefs about sex, open minded to new beliefs, trauma release to improve sexual relations, ect..
- Social and community Relationships-neighbors, meeting new people, filtering out old social and community relations, expanding into new circles of connecting, ect..

Take some time to do a self evaluation of these and any other areas in your life. Score yourself 1-10 on where you are at right now with your investments in the relationships of your life. Perhaps you will see some areas to spend a lot less time and attention on and re-invest that time and attention on new and different areas of your relationships. The relationships we invest the most time and attention to will flourish the most!

Write down a few changes of investments that you would like to make.

_____
_____
_____
_____
_____
_____

Under Pressure

"You don't know what you have until you have it under pressure".

This has been the most valued quote in all of my horsemanship and now in my humanship! Pressure is where change is made. Pressure is required for change. No pressure, no change. Pressure is the "*hard thing*" whatever that is in life, sometimes it's a hard thing to just get out of bed and go to the store, other times it's the hard thing to do a 2 minute ice bath. It's the decisions we make while under pressure that matter the most. Let's take the ice bath as an example. The ice bath never sneaks up on me and surprises me. . It's much more of a drawn out long slow process. First I have to create the opportunity for an ice bath, head into town to buy the ice, and fill up a horse water trough. Then make the conscious decision that "*I am Doing this!*" Step into the water at 34 degrees and sit down fully submerging yourself right up to your chin, remaining calm for 2 minutes. This is a struggle to say the least, my internal autonomic system is screaming "*YOU ARE GOING TO DIE!*" It is under this level of pressure that you find what you are really made of. Find your breath, quiet thoughts, focus on your breathing, all that matters is the calmness of your breathing. And then the quiet stillness overtakes you, you have mastered yourself, your autonomic system is now under your control instead of you being under its control, you feel absolute peace, stillness, you actually feel safe in the ice water. This is an amazing feeling, one that takes a great deal of struggle to get to. You see it never gets easy to get in the ice bath, it's a struggle every time, simply put, it gets easier for you to choose to do hard things. By creating experiences that we can take our "*new story*" into, to put our new story under pressure to prove that the new story is worthy, this is where we will make lasting neurochemical changes to our autonomic system. It's "*in the experience*" while under pressure that we prove our new story to create our new default neuro network of safety, to create the new version of SELF.

Creating New Version of Self

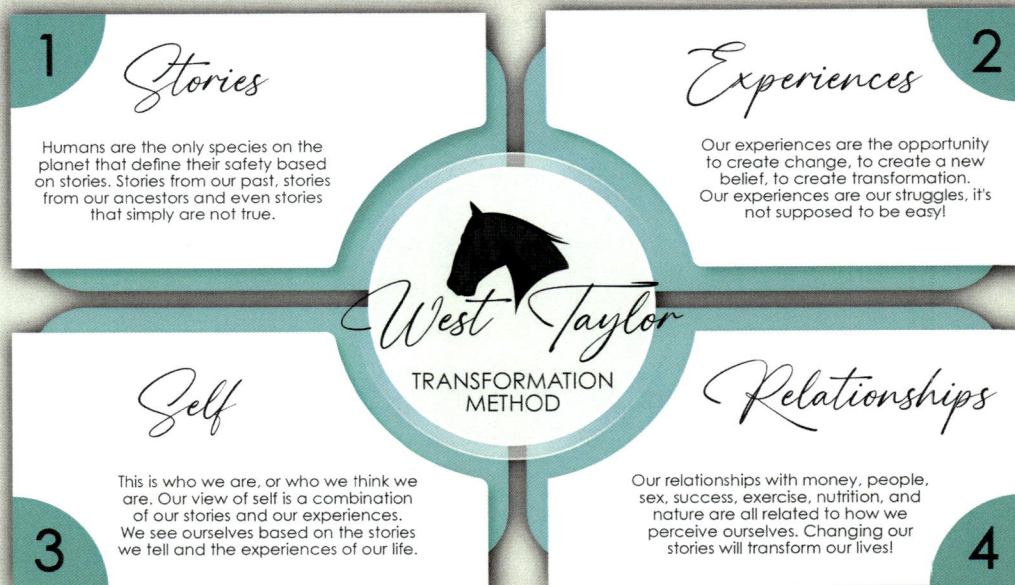

1 Stories

Humans are the only species on the planet that define their safety based on stories. Stories from our past, stories from our ancestors and even stories that simply are not true.

2 Experiences

Our experiences are the opportunity to create change, to create a new belief, to create transformation. Our experiences are our struggles, it's not supposed to be easy!

West Taylor
TRANSFORMATION METHOD

3 Self

This is who we are, or who we think we are. Our view of self is a combination of our stories and our experiences. We see ourselves based on the stories we tell and the experiences of our life.

4 Relationships

Our relationships with money, people, sex, success, exercise, nutrition, and nature are all related to how we perceive ourselves. Changing our stories will transform our lives!

Each time you find yourself having an experience that does not feel good or feels familiarly negative from previous experiences, this is your clue to pay attention and make some changes. What did you do last time you felt like this? What are you going to do this time to change the stories, to change the experience, to change self, to change your relationships? Your body is telling you through what it "*feels*". The big question is, are you listening?

Notes

Notes